WHAT YOU NEED TO KNOW ABOUT PROFESSIONAL BEHAVIOR

That Will Set You Apart From the Rest

Jeanne D. Maes | Linda Roussel

CENGAGE
Learning™

Australia • Brazil • Japan • Korea • Mexico • Singapore • Spain • United Kingdom • United States

WHAT YOU NEED TO KNOW ABOUT PROFESSIONAL BEHAVIOR: That Will Set You Apart From the Rest

Jeanne D. Maes I Linda Roussel

Executive Editor:
Maureen Staudt
Michael Stranz

Senoir Project Development Manager:
Linda de Stefano

Marketing Specialist:
Sara Mercurio
Lindsay Shapiro

Production/Manufacturing Manager:
Donna M. Brown

PreMedia Supervisor:
Joel Brennecke

Rights & Permissions Specialist:

Kalina Hintz
Todd Osborne

Cover Image:
Getty Images*

For product information and
technology assistance, contact us at **Cengage Learning Customer & Sales Support, 1-800-354-9706**

For permission to use material from this text or product, submit all requests online at **cengage.com/permissions**
Further permissions questions can be emailed to
permissionrequest@cengage.com

ISBN-13: 978-1-4240-8224-7

ISBN-10: 1-4240-8224-2

Cengage Learning
5191 Natorp Boulevard
Mason, Ohio 45040
USA

Cengage Learning is a leading provider of customized learning solutions with office locations around the globe, including Singapore, the United Kingdom, Australia, Mexico, Brazil, and Japan. Locate your local office at: **international.cengage.com/region**

Cengage Learning products are represented in Canada by Nelson Education, Ltd.

For your lifelong learning solutions, visit **www.cengage.com/custom**

Visit our corporate website at **www.cengage.com**

Printed in the United States of America

WHAT YOU NEED TO KNOW ABOUT PROFESSIONAL BEHAVIOR

That Will Set You Apart from the Rest

A Guidebook for Success on Your Job

Jeanne D. Maes

Linda Roussel

For our students

We hope that the material in this book will help you as you begin your careers.

Jeanne D. Maes

Linda Roussel

With thanks to the many people who have helped us with this project, and with special thanks to Mr. Abraham Mitchell for his contributions.

Foreword

Over the years that we have taught at the University of South Alabama, we have received many requests by our students (and former students) for information concerning the topic of professionalism. As a result, we have written this guidebook as a public service for you, our students.

The cost to you is the publisher's cost of printing. We receive no royalties whatever from the sale of this book.

We hope that the information you find in this book will help you as you begin your careers. We also hope that this is a book that you will want to keep as a handy quick-reference for the future.

Jeanne D. Maes, Ph.D.
Professor
Mitchell College of Business

Linda A. Roussel, DSN, RN
Professor
College of Nursing

Table of Contents

Appendix - A Brief History of the Professional Fields

The Importance of Professional Behavior in Today's Workplace

If you are in the workplace today, there is a standard of conduct that is expected – "professional behavior."

Professionalism is about serving others and the impression you leave on those you have served. It includes not only your expertise, competency, and skills but also your character, attitude, behavior, personal style, and dress.

In the years past, people took for granted that everyone knew, understood, and practiced professional conduct in the workplace. Professionals generally were raised in professional households and simply mimicked what they had seen and learned at home about acceptable conduct,

As the workplace has become more diverse, this expected standard of conduct has not always been understood or communicated. Many people in the workforce today were not raised in professional homes and, as a result, often do not know what professional conduct is. What previous generations took for granted, now requires training and education. (See the appendix for a brief history of the professional fields.)

Professional behavior has now become a more widely discussed issue. To illustrate, in October, 2003, entering the key words 'professional behavior' into Google, produced 3,960,000 links; in February, 2009, it produced 19,200,000.

Such an increase in links to information on professional behavior within such a relatively short period of time may be indicative of a number of issues. One thing is certain – behavior that was once taken for granted and understood as normal professional behavior, no longer is understood.   Moreover, it is rare in today's workplace for managers to take the time to explain it.

That is the purpose of this book - to give you a thorough understanding of "professional behavior" and what is expected when someone says, "You need to be more professional."

Professionalism: The Basics

An additional possible factor complicating an understanding of professional behavior is the seeming lack of a common or shared vocabulary.[i] Even if two individuals use the same word, they may hold totally different concepts of the word. Thus, if the meaning behind the word is not understood and embraced by both parties, there is no common vocabulary or shared meaning.

Today, the term professionalism includes:

1. The type of work that a person does (the field, the occupation), and

2. A set of standards regarding a person's behavior in work-related settings or situations.[ii]

There may be times on the job that you perform a task alone, are responsible for a piece of a larger task, or work in a team environment.

The outcome of any job is a showcase of your professionalism and focuses on of your <u>competence</u>. It highlights the amount of expertise that you bring to the job, the diligence with which you apply that expertise, and your concern for quality.

For example, you might be required to produce a report for your supervisor or for the Board of Directors. You demonstrate your skills and abilities in your research, your writing, your preparing updates, etc.

On the other hand, there will be times that you will be working with clients, patients, students, customers, or others within your organization to accomplish a job. Your interpersonal style, emotional intelligence, dress, timing, ethics, and integrity reflect your <u>character.</u>

For example, you may attend department meetings, call on customers, make presentations, provide bedside care for patients, etc.

Since professional behavior relates to both work and work-related settings, we offer the following examples along with helpful guidelines for your consideration.

There is good news. You can learn to be a true professional. It takes resolve, persistence, and time.

Examples, Please?

The following examples are real. The organizations and names of people involved have been changed to protect the guilty.

Example 1

A colleague once said, "Wouldn't it be great if we could just hire Sam's head and leave the rest of him at home?" While Sam was brilliant and had the skills that we needed to get the job done, working with Sam was anything but pleasant.

He sulked when he did not get his way; he personally attacked people in departmental staff meetings; he dressed like a real slob; he was habitually late; and, he bullied his way around the office. No one liked Sam, but his technical expertise was too valuable for the boss to fire him.

You can be sure that if the boss found someone who had Sam's technical knowledge and abilities but who was 'nicer' to people, the boss would replace Sam quickly.

Example 2

Sharon and Julie were college graduates. Both had earned master's degrees, and both were junior managers in the same organization. They were in their late 20s.

After six months on the job, they were invited to the chief executive officer's home for the annual Fourth of July company barbeque. When they asked about the dress code, they were told that it was 'casual.'

Sharon and Julie discussed with each other what to wear and even went shopping together for the right outfits. They appeared at the company function in halter tops with low bare backs, very short shorts, and sexy sandals. All of the other female employees wore crop pants and shirts with quarter-length sleeves.

The CEO's wife was shocked and spoke to the other executives' wives as well as her husband about Sharon and Julie's attire.

The next day, both Sharon and Julie were counseled for their lack of discretion at an official company event. Even after the 'counseling session,' neither of them really understood what the 'big deal' was.

Example 3

A high school teacher talked negatively to her class about another teacher and what the other teacher had done in a particular situation.

The negative discussion quickly spread around the school, and parents began calling the principal's office.

Things escalated. A few parents called the board of education and demanded that the teacher who was the subject of discussion be fired immediately. What the parents did not know was that none of the accusations were true. Everything had been a rumor started by the first teacher who had used poor judgment in talking publicly about a colleague.

Example 4

In a state agency department meeting a sensitive hiring issue was discussed. Topics brought up in the discussion were sent by email to other department members who could not attend the meeting.

Some of those receiving the emails sent blind copies of the message to other agency members outside the department. Threats of a lawsuit for defamation of character followed.

Example 5

A legal secretary and a law clerk were sent together on an errand for their firm. While shopping for office supplies, they were overheard discussing a very confidential legal matter.

The information was overheard by a friend of the defendant who relayed what he had overheard. This incident seriously jeopardized the outcome of the lawsuit.

Example 6

Hester, a supervisor, didn't want to do a particular task. "It's not part of my job description" he told his boss, even though the words in his job description stated "other duties as required and assigned."

A part of his professionalism was on the line. As a supervisor, you don't turn down tasks or refuse to perform a job assigned by the boss.

Example 7

A group of hospital staff went to lunch at the local café in a small rural community. A couple at the next table overheard their conversation about a particular patient's condition.

The patient was well known in the community and the patient's prognosis flew all over town within two hours after lunch as the rumor mill churned out stories – even before the family was notified of the diagnosis.

Example 8

After her probationary hiring period had passed, a female employee in a corporate office regularly began showing up for work in her long pink chenille bath robe, fuzzy slippers, and hair curlers. She clocked in and went straight to the restroom where she dressed, styled her hair, and applied her makeup.

She emerged from the restroom 45 minutes later looking like she had stepped out of *Vogue* magazine.

During the 45 minutes that she took to dress, her coworkers had to take all incoming telephone calls.

Needless to say, since the boss would not confront her about her lack of professionalism, morale sank to a very low level. Formerly loyal employees began to look for work in other companies.

Example 9

The members of a family construction company worked for several weeks gathering all the necessary data to put together a bid for a multi-million dollar, 24-month construction job in a large metropolitan city.

Son, an engineering graduate, who had been out of college for at least three years, grew up in the business. He had worked with Dad during high school, during summers when he was home from the university, and after his college graduation. Dad and Son worked together closely as a team.

This particular project was especially important to the family business as it would supply a lucrative income and assure work for at least two years. Dad emphasized that traffic conditions in this highly- congested metropolitan area dictated that Son would need to arrive at the bid site at least one hour ahead of the bid opening to submit his bid for the company.

Son arrived late – *less than five minutes late.* The bids were already open and Son was not allowed to submit his bid. He could only sit and listen as the authorized city official _posted_ the bids.

Dad's company would have been awarded the bid had Son been on time! To say that Dad was furious was an understatement!

Example 10

On a multi-million dollar public construction job, part of the architect's duty was to show where blocking, framing, and reinforcements need to be placed. (It is not unusual if the architect only shows an arrow where something needs to be mounted on a wall. This arrow alerts the contractor to work closely with the architect to make sure that the reinforcing is put at the correct location so that a plasma TV, for example, does not fall off the wall.)

On this particular complex project, with between 10 and 20 contractors on site at any given time, Contractor #2 discovered that Contractor #1 had not placed any reinforcing whatever in the entire building.

When confronted with this error, Contractor #1's response was, "That's not my job. It's

not part of my contract." He was wrong. It
was.

Example 11

Mary, a staff nurse on 5-East, was loved by
patients and families. They often asked to
be assigned to Mary when she was on duty.

Mary was attentive, caring and
compassionate when working with patients.
When patients told her that no one cared
like she did, and that the other nurses
assigned to them did not care, Mary began
to share staff issues and unit problems with
the patients.

She reported that many staff members were
"lazy, uncaring" and "didn't carry their
weight." Mary went on to relate that she
had reported these "goof offs" to her nurse
manager; however, nothing was ever done.
She believed that this was due to turnover
and the difficulty of keeping staff.

She suggested that "her" patients report
their complaints to the hospital
administration as she had repeatedly done
so without any changes. Mary told patients

that their dissatisfaction would be taken seriously and since she was "just a staff nurse," no one listened to her.

Example 12

Jean, a clinical nurse specialist on a surgical intensive care unit in a large medical center, prided herself in being a patient advocate. She strongly believed that health care providers should be "open and honest" with patients.

A patient on her floor was evaluated for pancreatic cancer. When the patient asked Jean to discuss test results with her, Jean did so, explaining that all diagnostic evaluation revealed that she had cancer. The patient was shocked by the results, began to scream at the staff, and throw things. She refused to talk to her family or her physician; she was inconsolable.

Jean was not aware that the patient's daughter had told the nurse manager and physician that it was important that her brother and sister be present when results were discussed. The daughter stated that her mother's history revealed a "hysterical" reaction to any "bad news."

When Jean was confronted by the family, she became defensive, stating that she was "taught" to always tell patients the "truth" no matter the circumstances.

Example 13

John was a nurse manager on a surgical-orthopedic unit. He regularly worked out at the gym 5-6 days per week. He was proud of his physical stature and wore snug- fitting shirts and slacks to work.

John had a number of tattoos on his upper arms which he generally "hid" with longer sleeves with his uniform. Lately, however, he wore shorter sleeves, exposing his body art.

When confronted by his immediate supervisor about his appearance, John stated that he had had his tattoos for a number of years and did not see this as an issue. In fact, he "resented" being confronted about this, stating "making an issue" of his body art was discriminatory.

He made his case and stated, "Steven has a large birthmark on his face and, to his knowledge, this had not been an "issue."

Example 14

Don was a new registered nurse in a small community hospital. While a student, Don received accolades from his faculty and clinical supervisors about his skillful techniques in delivering patient care.

After graduating, he took a position in a rural hospital in his hometown. While his skills at performing technical procedures such as giving injections, manipulating "tubes," etc. were excellent, he often ' talked down' to those reporting to him (unit secretary, patient care tech, etc.). The staff began to complain about him because they did not feel that Don respected them.

When his supervisor shared her concerns about the staff's complaints with Don, he shrugged it off stating that he was the registered nurse; in his position he had to "let people know who's in charge." He believed that without "showing who's boss," others would walk all over him. In his position, he could not afford to let this happen.

Example 15

Carol, a new registered nurse, accepted a job in a small nursing home in a rural area. During her first week's orientation, she was told that texting while on duty or talking on a cell phone, especially when with patient residents, was unprofessional and grounds for dismissal.

After three weeks on the job, Carol was caught talking on her cell phone to a friend. She was reminded by her supervisor about the penalty of talking on a cell phone while on duty.

Two weeks later, she was with a patient resident when her cell phone rang. Carol retrieved it from her pocket and began a conversation while attending the patient.

The patient complained to the nursing supervisor and Carol was terminated. Carol was shocked that she had been dismissed over such a small thing that had nothing to do with her technical skills.

Example 16

All employees, spouses, and significant others were invited to attend the retirement dinner party of a national company's district manager in a large southern metropolitan area. The atmosphere was quite casual and alcohol was served.

During the dinner, a number of managers and employees offered toasts to the retiring executive. One particular junior manager, a female in her early 30s, made her way to the podium to make her toast.

As her comments became slurred and increasingly inappropriate, the head of the human resource department was overheard to say, "Unacceptable and duly noted."

The woman's husband, a professional himself, was mortified as the large room suddenly got quiet and eyebrows were raised.

Some Guidelines[iii]

We offer the following as guidelines to help you think about your own current behavior. Place a checkmark by any that you believe merit your making personal adjustments.

1. Report to work on time.

2. Report to work dressed appropriately for the work and tasks that you will be doing.

If a uniform is not required for your job (as in the medical field), then you dress for the job that you <u>want</u>, not the one that you currently have.

Always dress in a way that will not send up a 'red flag' targeting you as a sexual harassment problem for your organization. In other words, if someone cannot stay focused on your face and your words, think carefully about your attire. (No 'skin-tight' clothing, low-cut shirts or blouses, or too-short skirts.)

If you are still unsure as to what is appropriate, take a good look at what and how those at the top of your organization wear their clothing and accessories.

Be sure to pay attention to your fingernails (clean and neat) and shoes (shined). Make sure that your clothes are clean and the wrinkles pressed out.

Remember that all company or organizational parties, picnics, fundraisers, events, galas, etc. are *business functions,* and these require appropriate business dress, even if the dress code is 'casual.' (Remember Example 2 – Julie and Sharon's experience.)

3. Report for work with an attitude that will allow you to have pleasant interactions with customers, clients, patients, students, coworkers, subordinates, or your boss.

In other words, leave all your irritations as well as being grumpy or angry (at the cat or the kids or the driver in the other lane or whomever) at home or somewhere else.

4. Report for work *alert* and ready to perform at your best *when you arrive*.

5. Accept that your boss or the particular job (or other) situation may determine when you must show up, when you can go home, how you dress for a particular task, and how you need to prepare to do the task.

6. Accept that your highest priority in service professions is to serve the patient, the customer, the client, etc.

Serving may mean more than the specific duties listed on your job description. For example, you may be a technical (or other) expert like Sam in Example 1, but if you make life on the job so unpleasant for others they will dread seeing you come to work – much less working with you.

7. Accept that you are part of a bigger picture in doing your organization's work, similar to a bolt in a machine that produces valuable products. Just as every piece of the machine is important for the machine to run efficiently, so *your* job is to do your part and cooperate with others who will be doing their parts to get the overall job done.

Viewing your job in this way will help you to see yourself in the right perspective as a team player; that is, *you* are not the center of attention or the main attraction. You are there to perform a service.

8. Give credit for a job well done or a good idea to the person, team or group to whom it belongs. Helping others excel also helps you.

9. Take full responsibility for your own actions, whether they are successes or failures.

This also means telling the truth about your actions even when you do not look so great because of it. These are called learning experiences.

10. Accept instructions, directions, and corrections from your boss or from others who have more expertise or knowledge than you do.

Learn from those who give you instructions, directions, or corrections, and, in turn, be willing to do the same for those less experienced than yourself.

11. Accept that your boss or your organization can direct you and instruct you in your tasks.

You may not always agree with your boss or your organization, but still carry out whatever you are instructed or directed to do as long as the customer, patient, client, etc. will benefit (and what you are being asked to do is not harmful, unethical, or illegal).

12. Respect other people's time as well as your own.

That means arriving on time for appointments and meetings. It also means that you do not waste other people's time. If you cannot come to a meeting or appointment, courteously call and let the others know that you cannot attend.

Additionally, when you are in charge of a meeting, begin the meeting at precisely the scheduled time so that you do not waste others' time. Let others know ahead of time the anticipated length of a meeting, and limit the discussion to fit into the allotted time frame and no later.

If the group did not accomplish everything on the agenda during the allotted time (and it is not an emergency meeting), schedule another meeting and list the unfinished items on the top of the agenda for the next meeting.

13. When you work in a team, always appreciate that at times you may lead the effort or serve as an enthusiastic follower.

14. Willingly share your feedback and do your part when you have been assigned to work in a team - or if you volunteer to do so.

15. Respect any resources that have been provided for you to do your job (and appreciate the fact that you have them). Use them *only* to do your job.

Some of these resources could be support staff (secretaries, file clerks, aides, runners, etc.); computers and/or technology; company cars and other transportation; cell phones, pagers, blackberries, etc.

16. Recognize that you are responsible for your own professional development and staying up-to-date in your field. Seek out special classes, workshops, books, software, etc. that enable you to continuously improve yourself and your performance.

Remember that in today's workplace, you manage your own career.

17. Recognize that you are responsible for your own job motivation. Focus on learning, achievement, recognition, rewards, and advancement as your motivators.[iv]

18. Show respect for others – whether clients, customers, patients, coworkers, etc. – by speaking in a courteous tone. Always speak positively (or not at all) about them to anyone else, such as in Example 3 about the classroom teacher.

19. Take responsibility for your own behavior.

Remember that others will respect you more if you acknowledge your own errors including poor performance and neglecting to perform.

Also remember that there is no place on the job for Drama Queens, those who throw tantrums, the helpless, the clueless, or whiners.

20. Be careful writing anything that could surface as a negative. Do not send anonymous notes, memos, or blogs that would be harmful to another person or to your organization.

When you respond to an email, text message, blog, or letter, be very careful what you say as well as how you say it. When in doubt, *don't!*

21. Cool down when you become angry or emotional and never put anything in writing when you are in such a state. Any negatively charged email messages to coworkers or clients with copies (blind or otherwise) to others are inappropriate.

If you have issues with another person, pick an appropriate time. Then go directly to that person and speak face-to-face. If the issue is not resolved, find what the appropriate channel is in your organization and go through that channel to settle the issue (not the email).

22. Agree to perform only tasks for which you know that you are prepared or qualified.

While you may enjoy challenges, realize that your performance affects others and you respect their right to have your best effort on their behalf.

23. Follow through when you agree to do something.

Meet deadlines (whether you have set them or someone else has).

Make sure that your work is always of the highest quality that you are capable of doing.

24. Remember that any time you are at lunch or dinner with a client, customer, coworker, vendor, etc. (or at any company or organizational event) to be careful with alcoholic beverages. (It is better to avoid them.)

Recognize that you must always be in control of your behavior (and your mouth).

25. Present a confident and upbeat view of your job to coworkers, customers, clients, patients, students, etc.; project a 'can-do' attitude.

A Few Essentials on Manners

What does the term 'manners' mean to you? Manners involve far more than how you hold a fork, how you introduce two or more persons, if you chew with your mouth open, or whether you talk on your cell phone in a crowded movie theatre.

Manners are all about how you treat other people. They are all about showing respect, human concern, and compassion for those you do not know well.[v] Moreover, manners can include simple things such as being kind, being considerate, being aware of another's presence and letting him/her pass in the hallway, or simply nodding or greeting someone.

Recently,[vi] the media has reported an epidemic of rudeness or lack of respect. Many believe that the anything-goes attitude of the Internet has contributed to this spreading lack of manners.[vii] It has certainly shown up in the workplace.

In a 2006 poll,[viii] 86% of respondents reported being "bothered a lot" by others who were rude and disrespectful; 75% reported being "bothered a lot by bad language." (They were not referring to bad grammar.)

Learning (and practicing) good manners should be a common sense matter; however, as shown above, with declining respect and rising rudeness, learning manners can be challenging.

An etiquette book is always useful; another very helpful way to become familiar with manners is to study the effects of people who regularly practice good manners.

Interpersonal Communication and Relations

We offer the suggestions below as some basics for the workplace.   Notice the human courtesy in each suggestion.

> Allow someone to finish his or her thought without interrupting – unless there is a real emergency.

> If there is ever a need to correct another person's grammar or pronunciation, do so privately.

> Show genuine interest in another person's good news – and don't burst someone else's balloon (by downplaying or ridiculing their happiness).

> Accept compliments gracefully.

> Ask others about *their* interests, accomplishments, etc. and discuss them more than your own.

Know when to "talk business" and when it is time to stop. In other words, be aware of others' body language and the clues they are sending you.

Practice being tactful. If there is a kinder way to say something, think about it and say it that way.

Certain topics are not always good (or smart) for conversation in professional settings. Remember who may be listening. Some of these topics include:

- Personal health details

- Details of someone else's health

- Controversial subjects such as religion, politics, sex, family problems, or anything overtly offensive

- How much something (personal) costs

- Personal misfortunes

- Stale, corny, worn-out subjects

- Any story that might be problematic, uncertain, or of questionable judgment

- Harmful gossip

Consider some of these examples:[ix]

"Is it true that you're losing your job?"

"Are you in therapy?"

"Tell me about _____ (the diagnosed disease) or about your divorce."

"How much do you weigh?"

"How old are you?"

"Have you had plastic surgery?"

"Do you color your hair?"

"Do you wear a wig (or a "rug")?"

"Is it true that you are a _____ (religious preference)?"

"Is it true that you are gay?"

Some Tips on Telephone Manners

Always identify yourself and your department.

Answer in a pleasant tone. Speak clearly and in a way that other people can understand all of your words.

When leaving a message for someone, speak slowly and distinctly. Be sure to slowly repeat your call back number.

When you are talking on the phone, do not chew gum or eat.

Be willing to offer help.

Be aware of and control noises in the background.

Remember to wait until you leave the restroom to talk on your cell phone. (Some things are very private!)

Always keep your cool!

Apologize if you reach a wrong number. Never just hang up!

Get to your point quickly; this does not waste the caller's time or yours.

When speaking with someone on the phone, sometimes it is helpful to "number" your points. Consider the following examples:

> "I'd like to talk to you about two issues."

> "In summary, I would like to leave you with three points."

Always remember to address clients, patients, etc. by their last name. Utilizing a person's formal name, until you are invited by the person to use the familiar (first) name, is a sign of respect.

> For example, you might say, "Hello Mrs. Green. I will be working with you today."

If your call is urgent and the party whom you are calling is not available, explain your business to the secretary.

Make your phone calls to someone (in your time zone) after 7:00 a.m. or before 9:00 p.m. unless that individual has requested that you do so. Remember to consider time zone differences when making phone calls outside your region.

Give your full attention to the other party on the line. Do not be reading email or texting or doing something else.

If you are in someone's office and they receive a telephone call, step out of the office to allow the person some privacy with the call.

If someone is in your office and you receive a telephone call, have the secretary take a message (if you have a secretary); if you do not have a secretary and you are not expecting an important call, let the caller leave a voice message and give full attention to the person in your office.

If someone is in your office and you receive an important telephone call, ask the party to excuse you and to please step out of your office for a moment while you take the expected call.

Some Tips on Table Manners

Table manners tell a lot more about you than your skills at using the correct fork, knife, spoon, and glasses. Table manners are about being considerate of other people.

You can be sure that you are being carefully watched if you are invited to have a lunch or dinner interview. Below are some basics (for manners in the United States) that you should know and practice. Remember that manners are cultural and change, depending on your companions.

1. Wash your hands before sitting down.

2. When you sit down, place you napkin in your lap.

3. Sit up straight and do not slouch.

4. Before ordering your food, listen to what others order. It's not a good

idea to order the most expensive item on the menu.

5. Ask politely for dishes to be passed; do not reach across the table.

6. Wait until everyone is served before you start to eat.

7. Remember that food is not a play-toy.

8. Keep your elbows off the table while eating.

9. Pass the salt and pepper shakers together.

10. Chew with your mouth closed and remember not to smack.

11. Talk only when you have swallowed your food, never while you are chewing.

12. Wipe your mouth frequently with your napkin, not your sleeve.

13. Use your knife, fork, spoon, glass, or cup without slamming or banging them on the plate or table.

14. Place your knife softly on the upper right edge of your plate when not in use.

15. Use a butter knife, if you have one.

16. Butter goes on your bread plate, if you have one; it goes on your dinner plate if you do not have a bread plate, and the butter knife stays with the butter.

17. Ask to be excused if you must leave the table.

18. Refrain from talking on your cell phone or text-message while at

the table. If you receive an important call and must take it, ask to be excused. Better yet, leave the phone in the car.

19. Start with your utensils (fork, spoon, and knife) and work from the outside to the inside. The same applies to glassware.

20. Enjoy what others have to say during your meal and do not dominate the meal conversation.

Remember – if you do not practice your manners every day, you will forget when you are in situations in which others are evaluating you!

Interviewing Tips

While you can always access the latest information regarding interviewing on the Internet, there are certain things that do not change. Observing these practices can set you apart from your competition.

1. Arrive on time or be a little early. This ensures that if you are caught in traffic, you will not have to worry.

2. Answer any questions clearly, articulately, and concisely. Think before you speak.

   Remember to be positive.

3. When asked about yourself, tell less than you think they ought to know.

4. Answer questions with brief explanations rather than a mere 'yes' or 'no.'

5. Sit up straight and be still in your chair. Squirming sends an undesirable message.

   Remember not to chew gum, tap your feet, wiggle your leg, or fidget, etc.

6. Remember to do your homework before you arrive. Learn as much as you can about the company and make notes. Bring these notes with you to

the interview. Include any questions that you want to ask the interviewer.

You can learn about a company or organization through Career Services, the Internet, the library, through people you know who may work there, etc.

7. Bring an extra copy of your resume and/or application. Also bring extra copies of your references (separate from your resume).

8. Buy the best clothing that you can afford in a classic style. If you are not sure what to wear, tell the salesperson that you have an upcoming job interview. He or she can help you select an appropriate suit, tie, shoes, etc.

For men, a coat and tie are usually appropriate.

For women, a suit is usually appropriate. Remember to wear sleeves and hose. Also remember that the less jewelry, the better (no dangling earrings, bracelets, etc.).

For both men and women, we suggest that you do not wear perfumes, colognes, or any fragrances. Too many people are allergic to them. Additionally, the sense of smell is a strong link to memories. (Their memories of similar smells may not be to your best interest.)

9. Turn off your cell phone during your interview. You can talk on your cell and text after the interview.

10. Remember to speak to all the staff persons as you enter. There have been numerous times that the entire staff has had the opportunity to voice an opinion of a candidate's interaction in the hiring decision.

This is especially true of the secretary. Sometimes this person can open doors for you.

11. At the end of the interview, stand up, extend your hand, and thank the

interviewer for his or her time. Ask when you might expect to hear a decision.

12. When you have shaken hands, it is time to leave. Do not over stay your welcome.

13. Write a thank you note within the week after your interview. This should be done whether you had a favorable interview or if you thought the interview went poorly.

14. Make sure that the greeting message on your cell phone or answering machine is appropriate and sounds professional.

15. Make sure that the email address listed on your resume is professional. Never use something like toughguy@gmail.com or beachbabe@yahoo.com.

16. Make sure that the car you take to the interview does not have any inappropriate bumper stickers. Candidates who have interviewed f

favorably have lost hiring opportunities for these.

17. Remember that employers check Facebook, MySpace, Twitter, etc.

As of September, 2008, at least 22% of employers were checking your Facebook and MySpace profiles when they are looking to hire you.[x]

The Stanford Daily News, in a January 20, 2006, article, reported a similar finding.   Stanford's Director of the Career Development Center, Lance Choy, 'confirmed that employers routinely conduct Web searches to find background information on job candidates… (including the use of Facebook)."

Choy went on to warn students, "Be careful about the image you portray in any public domain. You don't know who could be watching."[xi]

A View from the Top: How Your Boss Sees Things

If you can learn to think about work and performance from your boss' viewpoint, this will help you see what is important to your organization. It will help you to adjust your behavior and polish your skills.

Remember that your boss usually reports to someone else and is under pressure to perform just as you are. You want to make your boss and those with whom you work look good. Find what people do well and focus on that talent.

Think about what your boss needs and how you can help to make his or her job easier. You will become more valuable in the process.

In business (and most other organizations), results or outcomes are measured. Those measures, in turn, are used to make decisions. Your performance impacts those measures.

A director of manufacturing of a Fortune 500 Company recounted something that her boss had once said, "I hire people who know how to think, who have good ethics, and who have good morals. I can teach them the rest."

He also told her on another occasion, "If you don't make dust, you'll eat dust." In other words, if you don't take the initiative, someone else will outpace you.

At a recent health-care conference, one of the presenters, a dental school dean, told the audience that those students 'making the cut,' have good grades, high entrance exam scores, etc. When he considers applicants seeking to enter his dental school, he wants to know what they have done for their community. He often asks, "Did you build a house? Work with Boys and Girls Clubs? Since you would not likely apply if your grades were low, all applicants are generally smart, and possibly teachable. So, what sets you apart from the others?"

He stated that the qualities of community service, altruism, and compassion cannot be taught; if one does not "bring" them into the school or work setting, it is unlikely that they will be learned or developed there.

Another aspect of your professionalism is your emotional intelligence. (Emotional intelligence –or EQ - is the ability or skill to identify, evaluate, and manage your emotions – and those of others.[xii]) EQ has become a hot topic in today's workplace, and has produced continuing discussion about a person's ability to work with others and be a good team player.

Professional Socialization

When you accept a job in your area of expertise (your major), others in your field expect you to blend into the profession. That is called socialization.

Moreover, when you enter your chosen field and begin the socialization process, you make a commitment that basically says you will be the best that you can be. Many professions articulate which competencies they expect in their members.

For example, in the process of identifying the competencies necessary to the nursing profession, the O'Neil and Pew Commission on Nursing Socialization considered changes in society, changes in healthcare financing, and healthcare reform. Among the competencies identified were:

- Embracing a personal ethic of responsibility and service

- Exhibiting ethical behavior in all professional activities

- Contributing to the continuous improvement of the healthcare system

- Continuing to learn and help others.[xiii]

Helpful Self-Activities for Developing Professional Behavior

Below are several exercises that will help you to develop your professional behavior.

Activity 1

- Track your use of time for a week, keeping a log. At the end of the week evaluate how you spent time and identify ways to improve time management.

Consider:

- Why is time management important to you?

- How can working on personal time management make a difference professionally?

Activity 2

- Identify one study skill that you think you need to improve.

- Develop a plan for improvement.

Activity 3

- Attend a local professional organization meeting.

- Summarize what you learned at the meeting.

Activity 4

- Set up teams for learning activities in this book.

- Discuss how the team works and roles that team members take.

Activity 5

- Use examples from work you have done with teams in the past, such as in other courses, in student groups, even in high school, in social groups, and so on.

- Discuss these examples and their implications for team work.

It's Not Always *WHAT* You Say,

But *HOW* You Say It

You can learn from the master workers or experts (see Appendix) while working with members of different generations in your workplace.

As you do, you will find that you can get along with all of them! The key to doing so is being respectful of "where people are." The following information may give you some insights on how to work with them.

It's good to keep in mind that the events and conditions of our formative years help define who we are and how we view the world. That means that the 'formative' years, usually from birth to age 14,[xiv] is <u>one</u> important influence on our behavior as adults.

According to some sources, there are four generations currently in the workplace.[xv] They include:

1. Traditionalists/ the Silent Generation (born 1922-1943)

2. Baby Boomers (born 1943-1960)

3. Generation X/Thirteenth/ "Me Generation" (born 1960-1980)

4. Generation Y/Millenials/ Nexters (born 1980-2000)[xvi]

These generations are often stereotyped or categorized in certain ways. The following describes each generational group, its significant formative events, its values and its world-views.[xvii]

1. Traditionalists/ the Silent Generation (born 1922-1943).[xviii]

Described as the 'adaptive' generation, they were born and raised during the Great Depression. They experienced World II, the New Deal, and the Korean War.

They value:

- Hard work

- Dedication and sacrifice

- Respect for rules

- Duty before pleasure

- Honor

As a generation, they tend to be conformists, practical, dedicated, respectful, adhere to the hierarchy, conservative in their spending habits, past-oriented, and emphasize logic.

2. Baby Boomers (born 1943-1960).[xix]

Described as 'idealists, they were born and raised during an era in which the following occurred: the Women's Liberation Movement, the Civil Rights Movement, the Sexual Revolution, the Cold War, prosperity and suburbia, the space race, television, Vietnam, and the Kennedy and King assassinations.

They value:

- Optimism

- Teamwork and consensus

- Personal gratification

- Health and wellness

- Personal growth

- Working with youth

- Involvement

As a generation, they tend to be driven, soul-searching, willing to go beyond what is expected, and have a 'love-hate relationship' with authority.

3. Generation X/Thirteenth/ the 'Me' Generation (born 1960-1980).[xx]

Described as 'reactive,' they were born and raised during an era in which the following occurred: the Women's Liberation Movement (continued from the previous generation), Watergate, greenmail, Wall Street turmoil, the fall of the Berlin Wall, stagflation, latchkey kids, single parents, MTV, AIDS, personal computers, the Challenger disaster, glasnost, and Desert Storm.

They value:

- Diversity

- Thinking globally

- Techno literacy

- Fun and informality

- Balance

- Self-reliance

- Pragmatism

As a generation, they tend to be family-oriented, risk-takers, skeptical, unimpressed with authority, view the boss as a colleague, are reluctant to commit, and job-focused rather than work-hour focused.

4. Generation Y/Millenials/ Nexters (born 1980-2000).[xxi]

Described as 'civic,' they were born and raised at a time during which the following occurred: school shootings, the Oklahoma City bombing, Clinton/Lewinsky, internet chats, TV talk shows, multiculturalism, the girls' movement, attacks on the World Trade Center (1993 and 2001), the Gulf War, Iraq and Afghanistan.

They value:

- Civic duty

- Confidence

- Achievement

- Diversity

- Morality

- Social ability

- Street-smarts

As a generation, they tend to be tenacious, optimistic, and prefer cooperative action.

Generational Information - Applications[xxii]

To give you some ideas on translating this information into practical behaviors, we have retrieved the following material from Duke University's Office of Institutional Equity website.[xxiii] You may find additional useful information there.

Traditionalists and Baby Boomers

Individuals in these generations may have a tendency <u>not</u> to question or challenge authority (or the state of affairs that currently exists).

To the GenXer and GenYer, their lack of questioning may cause confusion and even resentment. GenXers and GenYers/ Millenials have been taught to speak up, challenge, and get 'in your face.'[xxiv]

Generation X and Generation Y

GenXers and GenYers communicate differently. They may fail to actively listen to Boomers and Traditionalists. In their not listening well, they may well miss valuable information and needed guidance (and tick off Boomers and Traditionalists in the process).

Issues with Feedback

Since effective communication is vital to workplace success, how you receive and give feedback can make all the difference in your interpersonal relationships.

Consider the following examples, taken from the webpage of the Office of Institutional Equity, Duke University.[xxv]

>Traditionalists – "No news is good news."

> Baby Boomers – "Give feedback once a year and keep lots of documentation."

> GenXers – "Hey, sorry to interrupt but how am I doing? And, by the way, I need to know <u>now.</u>"

> GenYers/Millenials – "I want feedback whenever I want it. That means at the push of a button."

Remember that feedback styles that may appear informative and helpful to one generation might seem formal and like a lecture or "preachy" to another.

For example, feedback that a GenXer thinks is immediate and honest can seem rushed and even tasteless to other generations.

Traditionalists and Boomers have been told that there is a time and place for feedback. GenXers and GenYers/Millenials have not necessarily been taught this 'expectation.'

Traditionalists may not seek public recognition or praise but they appreciate being recognized that they have 'made a difference.'

Baby Boomers often give feedback to others but seldom receive it themselves- especially positive feedback.

GenXers need positive feedback to let them know they're on the right track. Moreover, they need to hear it regularly.

GenYers/Millenials are accustomed to being praised. They may easily mistake someone's silence, hearing no feedback at all, or delayed feedback as disapproval. They need to know exactly what they're doing right and exactly what they're doing wrong.   In fact, they need a list with examples, and they need it <u>now</u>.

A Final Note

Behaving professionally does <u>not </u>mean that you have to be a stuffed shirt (quietly reserved) with no sense of humor. It does <u>not</u> mean being overly serious and never smiling. It does <u>not</u> mean that you cannot joke around or have fun.

A sense of humor – which includes learning to laugh at yourself - builds relationships. It is part of what life is all about.

It <u>does</u> mean that you know when it is okay to have fun or joke around and when it is time to be serious. Situation and timing are your keys.

Remember that becoming a professional is a journey, and no one is perfect. As you apply the suggestions outlined in this book, you will find yourself on the way to becoming a master worker (mentioned in the appendix).

Enjoy your journey!

---

[i] James B. Richards, *Anatomy of a Miracle.* (Orrstown, PA: Milestones International Publishers, 2009), p. 26.

[ii] Cornelius Grove and Willa Hallowell, (2002 3rd quarter), "The Seven Balancing Acts of Professional Behavior in the United States, A Cultural Values Perspective," *Focus*

Europe, a supplement to *Velocity*, the magazine of the Strategic Account Management Association (3rd quarter, 2002). Retrieved from website on December 14, 2008: http://www.grovewell.com/pub-usa-professional.html.

[iii] Many of these examples have been adopted from Michael Chial, "Viewpoint: Conveying Expectations about Professional Behavior," *Audiology Today,* vol. 10, no. 4, p. 25.

[iv] Mike Austin, Executive in Residence, Mitchell College of Business, Organizational Communication guest lecture, Fall, 2007.

[v] WikiHOW, 'How to Have Good Manners." Retrieved from website March 2, 2009: http://www.wikihow.com/index.php?title=Have-Good-Manners&printable=yes.

[vi] John Cohen and Gary Langer, "Poll: Rudeness in America, 2006." Retrieved from ABC News website on March 2, 2009:

http://abcnews.go.com/2020/US/story?id=15
74155.

[vii] Janet Kornblum, "Rudeness, threats make
the Web a cruel world." Retrieved from
USAToday website on March 2, 2009:
http://www.usatoday.com/tech/webguide/int
ernetlife/2007-07-30-cruel-web_N.htm.

[viii] John Cohen and Gary Langer, "Poll:
Rudeness in America, 2006." Retrieved
from ABC News website on March 2, 2009:
http://abcnews.go.com/2020/US/story?id=15
74155.

[ix] Material adapted from Letiticia Baldridge's
*New Manners for New Times (*New York:
Scribner, 2003*)*.

[x] Vasanth Sridharan, "22% Of Employers
Check Your Facebook Profile When They're
Looking To Hire You. That's It?" (September
14, 2008). Retrieved from website on April
2, 2009:
http://www.businessinsider.com/2008/9/22-
of-employers-check-your-facebook-profile-
when-they-re-looking-to-hire-you-that-s-it-.

[xi] Andrea Fuller. "Employers Snoop on Facebook," *The Stanford Daily News* (January 20, 2006). Retrieved from website on April 2, 2009: http://daily.stanford.edu/article/2006/1/20/employersSnoopOnFacebook.

[xii] Adapted from the definition given in Wikipedia and EQI. Retrieved from websites on March 8, 2009: http://en.wikipedia.org/wiki/Emotional_intelligenceed and from http://eqi.org/eidefs.htm.

[xiii] E. N. O'Neil and the Pew Health Profession Commission (1998). Recruiting health professional practice for a new century. (San Francisco: Pew Health Professions Committee.)

[xiv] According to Douglas Adams, author of *The Hitchhiker's Guide to the Galaxy,* anything that is in the world when you were born is 'normal' and is the way the world works. Anything invented between ages 15-35 is 'new, revolutionary, and exciting.' You might even find your career here. Anything

invented after you are 35 is 'not normal.'
Cited from N. Boyce Appel, President, Appel
Associates, "Management Breakfast:
Generational Differences and Implications
for Human Resources," *AIA Practice
Management Digest* (Spring 2009).
Retrieved from website on March 29, 2009:
http://info.aia.org/nwsltr_pm.cfm?pagename
=pm_a_20030801_breakfast.

[xv] "Cross Generational Communication,"
Office of Institutional Equity, Duke
University, 'PowerPoint presentation.
Retrieved from website on September 4,
2007:
http://www.duke.edu/web/equity/Diversity_e
duOpp.htm.

[xvi] Cited from N. Boyce Appel, President,
Appel Associates, "Management Breakfast:
Generational Differences and Implications
for Human Resources," *AIA Practice
Management Digest* (Spring 2009).
Retrieved from website on March 29, 2009:
http://info.aia.org/nwsltr_pm.cfm?pagename
=pm_a_20030801_breakfast.

[xvii] "Cross Generational Communication," Office of Institutional Equity, Duke University, 'PowerPoint presentation. Retrieved from website on September 4, 2007: http://www.duke.edu/web/equity/Diversity_eduOpp.htm.

[xviii] Adapted from N. Boyce Appel, "Generations: Dealing with Boomers, Gen-X, and Beyond," *AIA, Practice Management Digest* (Spring 2009). Retrieved from the Web, March 29, 2009: http://info.aia.org/nwsltr_pm.cfm?pagename=pm_a_20030801_genx.

[xix] Ibid.

[xx] Ibid.

[xxi] Ibid.

[xxii] Taken from Cross Generational Communication," Office of Institutional Equity, Duke University, 'PowerPoint presentation. Retrieved from website on September 4, 2007:

http://www.duke.edu/web/equity/Diversity_e
duOpp.htm.

[xxiii] Ibid.

[xxv] Ibid.

Appendix

A Brief History of the Professional Fields

Around 1900, in the United States, only three occupations were recognized as professions. These were law, medicine, and theology.[i]   At that time in history, most women did not work outside the home; therefore, most of these fields were dominated by men.

Because there were few specialized schools to train doctors, attorneys, and ministers, most of them learned as apprentices - similar to mentoring or internships in today's workplace.

The growth process from apprentice to accomplished professional was often quite lengthy. It took time to develop the requisite knowledge and skills to develop competency.

The apprentice professional learned by watching the expert and working beside him. Not only did the apprentice learn the specific work itself, but also style, timing, and rhythm.

By 1930, additional lines of work such as engineering and accounting had been added to the list of recognized professions. These professions were also dominated by men, and the collective behaviors of their members became the norm.

With the start of World War II, many women began to work in factories to support the war effort at home. At the end of the war, some women continued to work, but the majority returned to more traditional roles of wives and mothers. This trend continued during the 1940s and 1950s.

The passage of the Civil Rights Act of 1964, coupled with the sexual revolution of that period, became a cultural turning point, paving the way for a diverse workforce and a change of perspective regarding the professions.

As these diverse groups entered the workplace, they brought the values and beliefs of their generations, molded by the events and trends of their formative years.[ii] Gradually, these various attitudes, values and beliefs have made their impact on the workplace.

Over the years since the 1930s, the number of recognized professions has grown. For example, as of April, 2009, in the State of New York alone there were 48 licensed professions, many of which were related to the medical fields. [For complete list, see this section's endnotes.[iii]]   All require licensure or certification.[iv]

In addition, the professions typically require the following:

- A specialized body of knowledge and skill; a sense of vocation;

- A set of minimum qualifications to enter the field and a certification and/or licensure that indicates legitimacy;

- A code of ethics and system of self-regulation;

- A means of sharing information among members of the profession; and,

- A concern for the greater good of society, more than just seeking compensation for members of the profession.[v]

In order to continue to meet the standards of any profession, members must continue to update their knowledge and document that specialized training by submitting continuing education units (CEUs) to their appropriate professional organizations.

In addition to those previously recognized, the range of occupations viewed as professions has widened significantly.[vi] There are now professional football players, professional basketball players, professional wrestlers, and those engaged in other sports; salon professionals, massage therapy professionals, and even professional truck drivers.

Moreover, the behaviors expected from members of each of these occupations vary significantly. It is no wonder that the definition of professional appears to be cloudy.

The Challenge Today

In the United States, when a professional is not successful, it may be due to a number of reasons. These reasons may range from a lack of technical expertise to having the necessary skills to perform; but it can also be due to a failure to act in ways that peers and counterparts expect.[vii] Thus, both character and competence are significant when we think of professionalism.

Misunderstanding the fine distinctions connected with the term 'professionalism' can also complicate life on the job – especially in the global workplace. This can be quite frustrating for those not raised or socialized in the United States[viii] since these expectations are rarely written in a job description or communicated explicitly.

Endnotes

[i] Many of these examples have been adopted from Michael Chial, "Viewpoint: Conveying Expectations about Professional

Behavior," *Audiology Today,* vol. 10, no. 4, p. 25.

[ii] According to Douglas Adams, author of *The Hitchhiker's Guide to the Galaxy,* anything that is in the world when you were born is 'normal' and is the way the world works. Anything invented between ages 15-35 is 'new, revolutionary, and exciting.' You might even find your career here. Anything invented after you are 35 is 'not normal.' Cited from N. Boyce Appel, President, Appel Associates, "Management Breakfast: Generational Differences and Implications for Human Resources," *AIA Practice Management Digest* (Spring 2009). Retrieved from website on March 29, 2009: http://info.aia.org/nwsltr_pm.cfm?pagename =pm_a_20030801_breakfast.

[iii] License Requirements/Application Forms, Office of the Professions, New York State Education Department. Retrieved from website on March 31, 2009: http://www.op.nysed.gov/proflist.htm.

List of Recognized Professions in New York State (requiring licensure or certification)

<u>Acupuncture</u>
<u>Architecture</u>
<u>Athletic Training</u>
<u>Audiology</u>
<u>Certified Shorthand Reporting</u>
<u>Chiropractic</u>
<u>Clinical Laboratory Technology</u>
· Clinical Laboratory Technologists
· Cytotechnologists
· Clinical Laboratory Technicians
· Certified Histological Technicians
<u>Dentistry</u>
· Dentists
· Dental Anesthesia/Sedation
· Dental Hygienists
· Certified Dental Assistants
<u>Dietetics-Nutrition</u>
<u>Engineering</u>
<u>Midwifery</u>
<u>Nursing</u>
· Registered Professional Nurses
  · Nurse Practitioners
· Licensed Practical Nurses

Occupational Therapy
· Occupational Therapists
· Occupational Therapy Assistants
Ophthalmic Dispensing
Optometry
Pharmacy
· Pharmacists
· Pharmacy Establishments
Physical Therapy
· Physical Therapists
· Physical Therapist Assistants
Interior Design
Land Surveying
Landscape Architecture
Massage Therapy
Medical Physics
Medicine
· Physicians
· Physicians, 3-year limited license
· Physician Assistants
· Specialist Assistants
Mental Health Practitioners
· Creative Arts Therapists
· Marriage and Family Therapists
· Mental Health Counselors
· Psychoanalysts

Podiatry
Psychology
Public Accountancy
· Certified Public Accountants
· Public Accountants
Respiratory Therapy
· Respiratory Therapists
· Respiratory Therapy Technicians
Social Work
Speech-Language Pathology
Veterinary Medicine
· Veterinarian
· Veterinary Technician

Note: Law is listed in another place and not on this website.

[iv]Ibid.

[v] Adapted from the following three sources: Sir Alan Langlands, "*Gateways to the Professions*" Report. Retrieved from website on March 31, 2009: http://www.dius.gov.uk/higher_education/widening_participation/gateways_to_the_profe

ssions/~/media/publications/Gateways_to the_Professions_Report.

License Requirements/Application Forms, Office of the Professions, New York State Education Department. Retrieved from website on March 31, 2009: http://www.op.nysed.gov/proflist.htm.

The Organization Development Institute, "Building the Field of Organization Development into a Profession." Retrieved from website on April 1, 2009: http://www.odinstitute.org/building.htm.

[vi] Michael Chial, "Viewpoint: Conveying Expectations about Professional Behavior," *Audiology Today,* vol. 10, no. 4, p. 25.

[vii] Cornelius Grove and Willa Hallowell, (2002 3rd quarter), "The Seven Balancing Acts of Professional Behavior in the United States, A Cultural Values Perspective," *Focus Europe, a* supplement to *Velocity*, the magazine of the Strategic Account Management Association (3rd quarter, 2002). Retrieved from website on

December 14, 2008:
 http://www.grovewell.com/pub-usa-professional.html.

viii Ibid.